RAINY DAYS
Arts & Crafts

JEWELLERY

DENNY ROBSON

WATTS BOOKS
London • New York • Sydney

CONTENTS

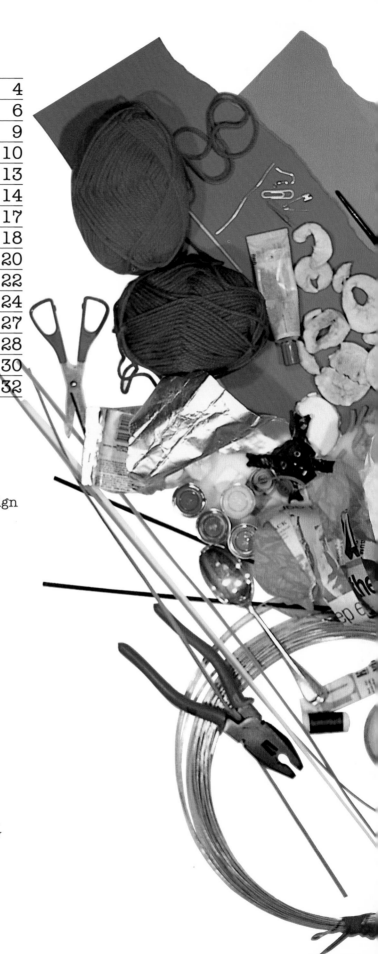

Design: David West
　　　　　　Children's Book Design

Designer
and jewellery: Keith Newell
Photography: Roger Vlitos

© Aladdin Books Ltd 1993

Created and designed by
N.W. Books
28 Percy Street
London W1P 9FF

First published in
Great Britain in 1993 by
Watts Books
96 Leonard Street
London EC2A 4RH

ISBN 0 7496 1304 1

A CIP catalogue record for this book
is available from the British Library

Printed in Belgium

Introduction

People have always worn jewellery and for many different reasons. Early hunters wore the teeth and bones of animals they had been brave enough to kill. Today soldiers are given medals to wear as evidence of their bravery. The chief of an early tribe might have worn a special decoration to show his importance. A high official today may wear a chain to show his status.

People may also wear jewellery to show off their wealth and for religious reasons. But most of us wear jewellery simply to decorate ourselves and because it's fun.

Making jewellery is a satisfying and enjoyable craft. Rings, brooches, necklaces, earrings, tie pins, hair ornaments.... this book gives you lots of jewellery-making ideas. As well as using the more traditional wire and clay, you can find out how to make your 'gems' from wool, dried fruit, pasta, pastry and even paper!

Here are some of the materials used to make the jewellery in this book. Most things are not expensive to buy and you may find much of what you need at home. Before you begin, check the materials needed and gather everything together. If the project involves gluing, painting or papier mâché, it's a good idea to cover your work surface with newspaper before you begin.

1

1 Draw your designs on to strong card and cut them out.

2

2 Cut a 'V' in the centre of each shape. This is what you use to attach the earring to your ear.

Card earrings

These clever earrings are very easy to make because they need no hooks or clasps. And what's more, they can be made to any shape, colour or design you choose.

You will need strong card, coloured paper, scissors, glue, coloured pens to decorate.

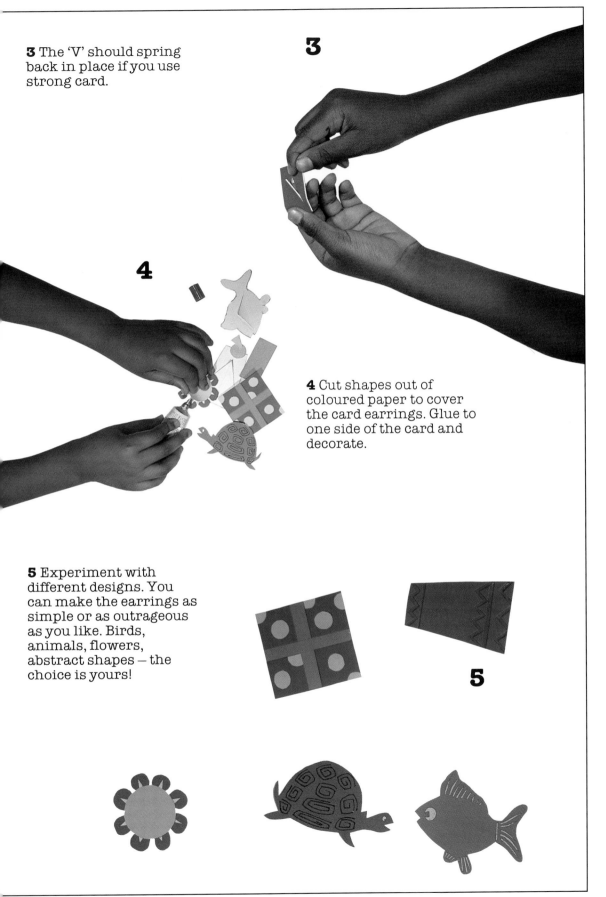

3 The 'V' should spring back in place if you use strong card.

3

4

4 Cut shapes out of coloured paper to cover the card earrings. Glue to one side of the card and decorate.

5 Experiment with different designs. You can make the earrings as simple or as outrageous as you like. Birds, animals, flowers, abstract shapes – the choice is yours!

5

Dried food jewellery

You can make unusual and effective jewellery from dried foods, like these matching earrings and necklace. Paint with clear varnish to get a strong, glossy finish.

You will need dried apple rings, dried macaroni, dried red kidney beans, needle and thread, earring hooks and wire (which can be bought at a craft shop or you can make your own — see page 28), paper clips, clear varnish, paint brush, pliers.

1

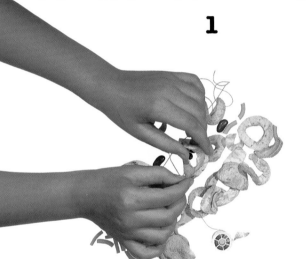

1 Use a needle and thread to string a few macaroni pieces together to make one end of the necklace, (see picture 3). Sew through the first apple slice as shown. Take care not to sew too close to the edge or the apple slice will break.

2 Next thread the needle through a piece of macaroni, then sew through another piece of apple. Continue to alternate macaroni and apple until the necklace is the required length.

2

3 Thread macaroni pieces to match the other end of the necklace. Tie each end to paper clips. The paper clips will link together to act as the fastener.

4 To make the earrings, push a piece of hooked wire (see page 28) through a kidney bean. You may have to try a few before you succeed as the beans may split.

5 Add a piece of macaroni and then push the wire into the apple slice. Bend the end of the wire to secure it. (This is best done with pliers.)

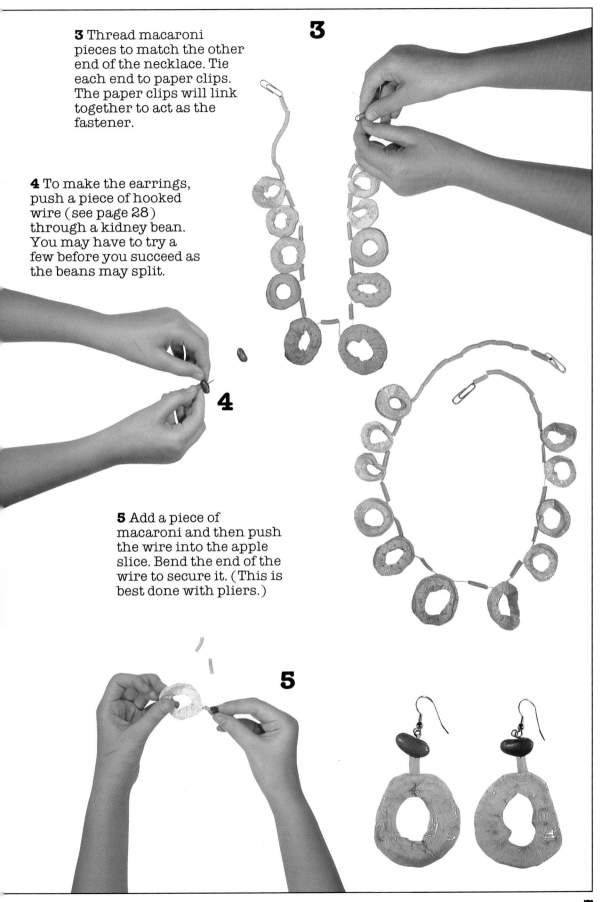

1 Heat the oven to 150°C (Mark 2). Put the flour and salt into a mixing bowl. Pour in the water, mixing all the time, so that you form a dough.

2 Knead the dough until it is smooth. Sprinkle flour on to your work surface and roll out the pastry.

3 Cut out the jewellery shapes, either by using pastry cutters, or make up your own shapes and cut them out with a blunt knife.

4 Use a palette knife to place the shapes on a non-stick baking tray. Bake until hard. This should take between 2-4 hours.

Pastry pieces

This jewellery is made from a clay-like dough of flour, salt and water. You harden the mixture by cooking it for a long time in a cool oven. It may look like pastry, but don't try to eat it — it would taste horribly salty!

You will need 750g salt, 750g flour, 500ml water, spoon, mixing bowl, rolling pin, shaped pastry cutters, palette knife, baking tray, paints, brush, clear varnish.

5

5 When the shapes are cool they can be painted. Wait until the paint is dry before you varnish them.

6 Thread string through a shape to make a necklace, or use sticky tape to fix a paper clip to the back to make a badge.

6

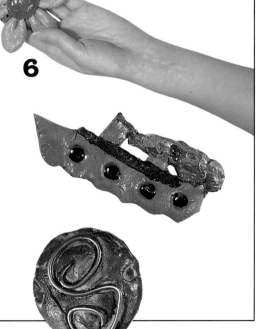

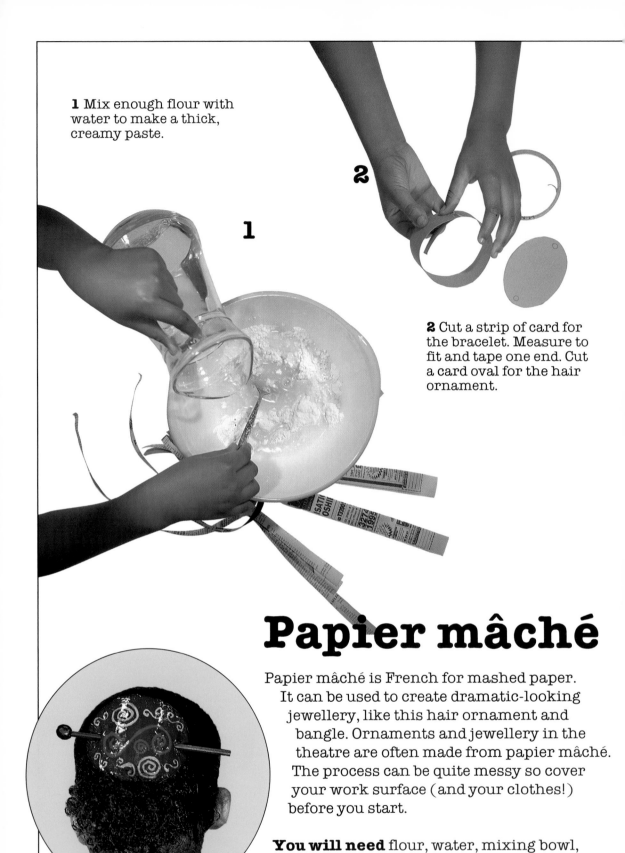

1 Mix enough flour with water to make a thick, creamy paste.

1

2

2 Cut a strip of card for the bracelet. Measure to fit and tape one end. Cut a card oval for the hair ornament.

Papier mâché

Papier mâché is French for mashed paper. It can be used to create dramatic-looking jewellery, like this hair ornament and bangle. Ornaments and jewellery in the theatre are often made from papier mâché. The process can be quite messy so cover your work surface (and your clothes!) before you start.

You will need flour, water, mixing bowl, spoon, strips of newspaper, card, scissors, sticky tape, thin garden cane, clay bead (see page 24), paints and varnish.

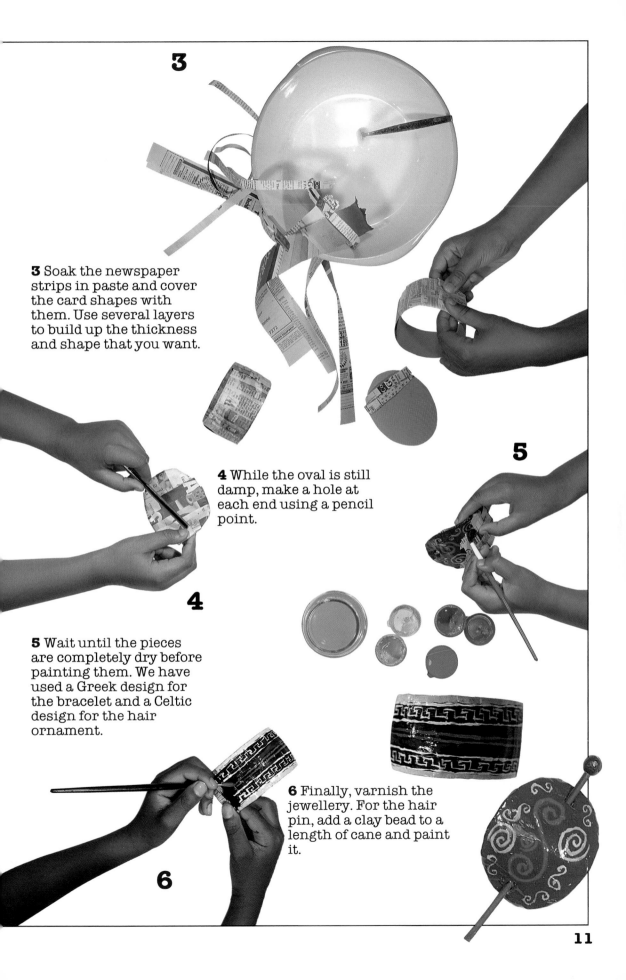

3

3 Soak the newspaper strips in paste and cover the card shapes with them. Use several layers to build up the thickness and shape that you want.

4 While the oval is still damp, make a hole at each end using a pencil point.

4

5

5 Wait until the pieces are completely dry before painting them. We have used a Greek design for the bracelet and a Celtic design for the hair ornament.

6 Finally, varnish the jewellery. For the hair pin, add a clay bead to a length of cane and paint it.

6

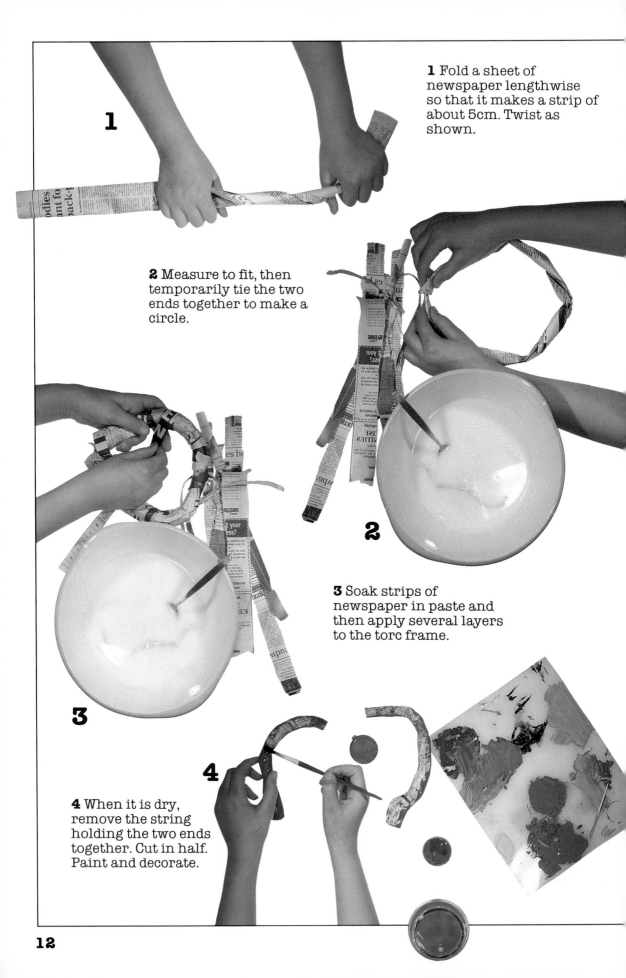

1 Fold a sheet of newspaper lengthwise so that it makes a strip of about 5cm. Twist as shown.

2 Measure to fit, then temporarily tie the two ends together to make a circle.

3 Soak strips of newspaper in paste and then apply several layers to the torc frame.

4 When it is dry, remove the string holding the two ends together. Cut in half. Paint and decorate.

Torc and tie-pin

Here we have used papier mâché to make a torc, which is a type of open necklace, and a tie-pin. Torcs were worn by the Celts as decorative jewellery, but originally they had a more sinister purpose. Wrapped around the neck, they could break the unsuspected blow of an enemy sword on the back of the neck.

You will need flour, water, mixing bowl, spoon, newspaper, card, scissors, string, cocktail sticks, paints, brush, varnish.

5 Use a cocktail stick to join the halves together. This allows you to twist the torc to put it on.

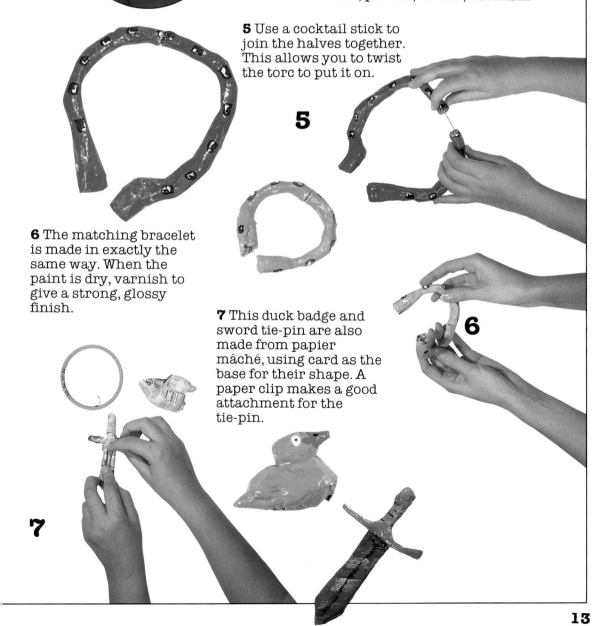

6 The matching bracelet is made in exactly the same way. When the paint is dry, varnish to give a strong, glossy finish.

7 This duck badge and sword tie-pin are also made from papier mâché, using card as the base for their shape. A paper clip makes a good attachment for the tie-pin.

1 From coloured paper cut a rectangle for the bird's body, a circle cut into halves for wings, a triangle for the beak, a fringed strip for the crest and two feet as shown.

1

2

2 Roll the rectangle into the shape of the body and glue. Glue the crest to the top.

3 Add the wings and feet. Fold the beak in half, open and glue to the centre of the body.

3

Bird earring

This crazy bird earring is an example of paper sculpture. Take some brightly coloured paper, add a little imagination and you can make a whole range of three-dimensional jewellery like this. The fish 'mobile' earrings are fun to make and wear.

You will need coloured paper, white paper, pen, scissors, glue, cocktail stick, paper clips, thread.

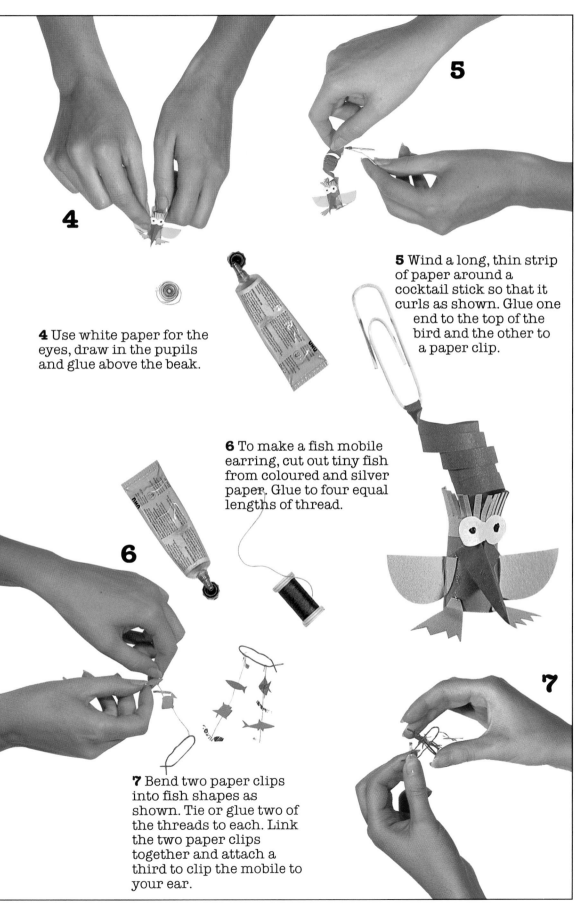

4 Use white paper for the eyes, draw in the pupils and glue above the beak.

5 Wind a long, thin strip of paper around a cocktail stick so that it curls as shown. Glue one end to the top of the bird and the other to a paper clip.

6 To make a fish mobile earring, cut out tiny fish from coloured and silver paper. Glue to four equal lengths of thread.

7 Bend two paper clips into fish shapes as shown. Tie or glue two of the threads to each. Link the two paper clips together and attach a third to clip the mobile to your ear.

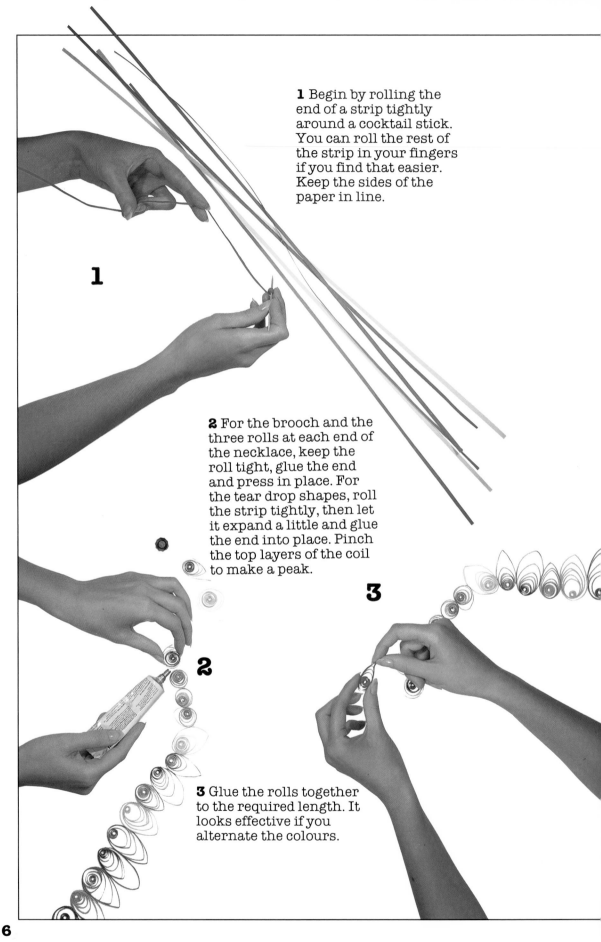

1 Begin by rolling the end of a strip tightly around a cocktail stick. You can roll the rest of the strip in your fingers if you find that easier. Keep the sides of the paper in line.

1

2 For the brooch and the three rolls at each end of the necklace, keep the roll tight, glue the end and press in place. For the tear drop shapes, roll the strip tightly, then let it expand a little and glue the end into place. Pinch the top layers of the coil to make a peak.

3

2

3 Glue the rolls together to the required length. It looks effective if you alternate the colours.

4 Glue a paper clip to each end of the necklace to act as a fastener.

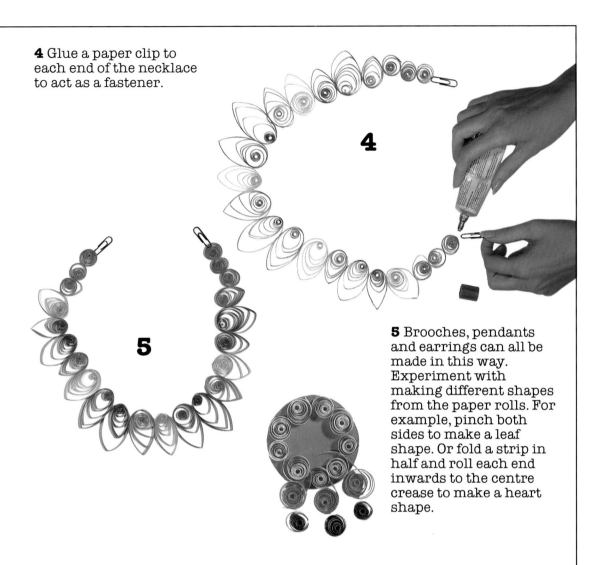

5 Brooches, pendants and earrings can all be made in this way. Experiment with making different shapes from the paper rolls. For example, pinch both sides to make a leaf shape. Or fold a strip in half and roll each end inwards to the centre crease to make a heart shape.

Paper filigree

This jewellery is made with paper filigree. Tiny rolls of paper are glued together to give an effect like lace. The craft of rolling paper is sometimes called quilling, because it was originally done on quills. It requires patience, but the results are very pretty, unusual and surprisingly strong.

You will need strips of coloured paper, cocktail sticks, glue, paper clips, card.

1 Copy shape 2 shown on page 32 with a pencil and ruler. Draw in the dotted lines and cut along the solid lines. Lightly score along the dotted lines with a ruler and scissors.

2 Fold up into a box shape, tucking in all the flaps. Close the box by tucking in the top flap.

3 Decorate as you wish and line with tissue paper.

Jewellery boxes

It's always nice to receive hand-made gifts, and when they come in unique boxes it's even better! Here are some different designs for jewellery boxes for you to make. You can make the boxes any size you like and decorate them with your own designs to make them truly original.

You will need thin card, pencil and ruler, scissors, glue, tissue paper, coloured pens, gummed shapes, glitter etc to decorate.

4 This jewellery box has a separate lid. Copy figure 1 shown on page 32. Draw in the dotted lines and cut along the solid lines. Fold in the tabs and glue.

4

5

5 Decorate and line with contrasting tissue paper to make the jewellery look more effective.

6 To make this ring box, copy figure 3 shown on page 32. Cut along the solid lines and fold along dotted lines.

7 Fold up the box and insert the card with the square cut from the centre.

6

7

8 To make this unusual pyramid jewellery box, copy and cut out the shapes shown in figure 4 on page 32. Fold along the dotted lines and glue the tabs.

8

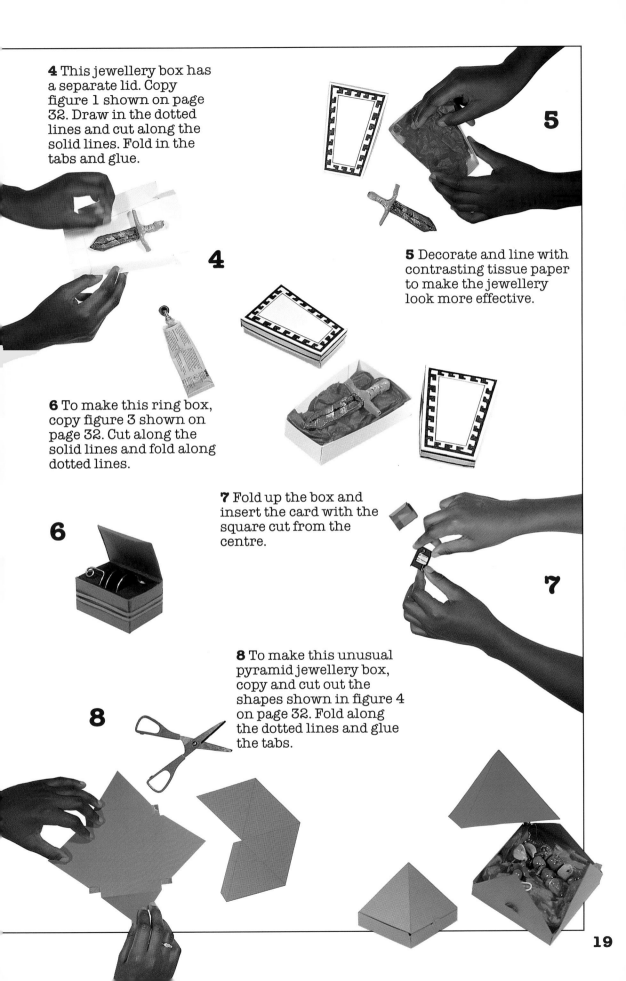

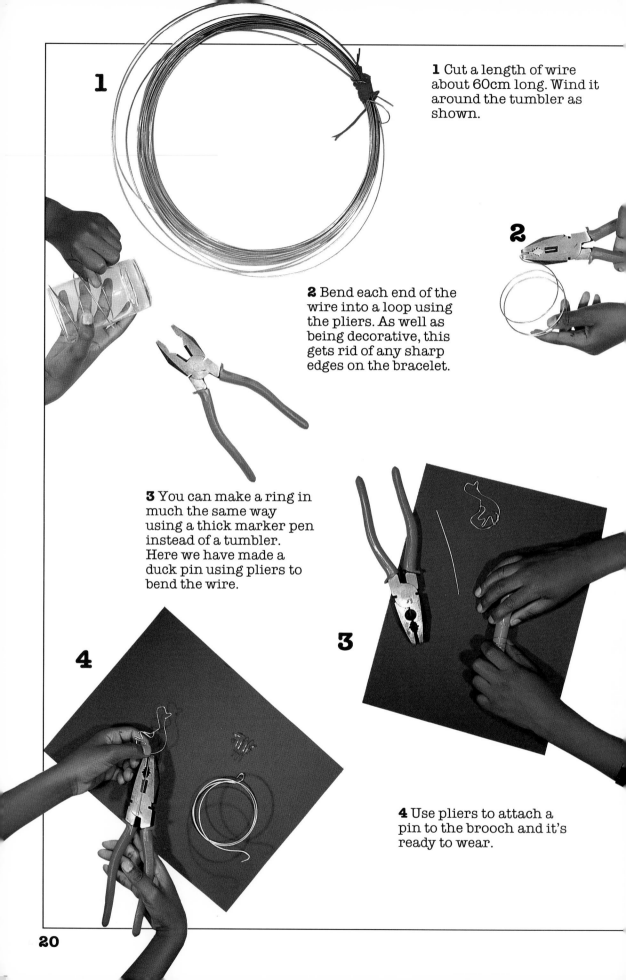

1 Cut a length of wire about 60cm long. Wind it around the tumbler as shown.

2 Bend each end of the wire into a loop using the pliers. As well as being decorative, this gets rid of any sharp edges on the bracelet.

3 You can make a ring in much the same way using a thick marker pen instead of a tumbler. Here we have made a duck pin using pliers to bend the wire.

4 Use pliers to attach a pin to the brooch and it's ready to wear.

5 Cut several pieces of wire long enough to bend around the tumbler. Make beads using non-bake clay and use to secure and cover the ends of the wire. Paint with enamel paints.

Wire wear

All the jewellery on this page is made from soft modelling wire, which is available from craft shops. You can bend this wire into lots of interesting shapes by just using your fingers. But to achieve precise effects you will find a pair of pliers very useful.

You will need modelling wire, flat pliers (preferably with smooth jaws so that they don't mark the metal), a glass tumbler, thick marker pen, wire cutters or scissors, enamel paints and paint brush, glue, clay for beads.

Pom-poms

Learning how to make pom-poms is useful for many crafts. You can make soft toys with them, decorations for clothes, or create even a mobile with them. Pom-poms make effective, fun jewellery. Use them for hair ornaments, earrings or turn them into funny brooches.

You will need card, wool, scissors, glue, safety pins, paper shapes to decorate the badges.

1 Draw two circles the same size on card and cut out. Cut out the circles in the centres as shown.

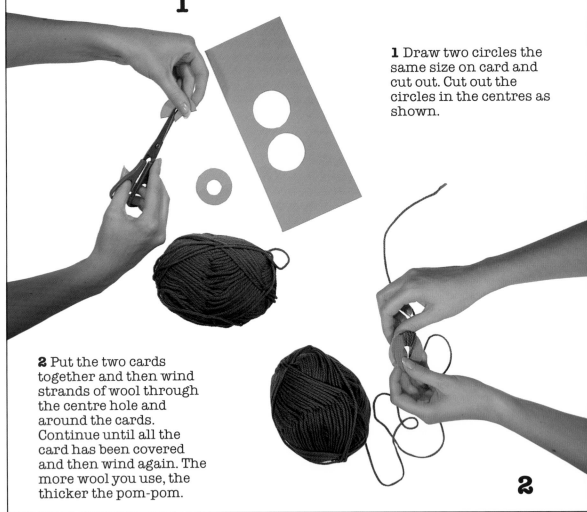

2 Put the two cards together and then wind strands of wool through the centre hole and around the cards. Continue until all the card has been covered and then wind again. The more wool you use, the thicker the pom-pom.

3 Carefully cut the wool around the edge between the two cards.

3

4 Slide a strand of wool between the two cards and tie it tightly to hold the wool together.

4

5 Tear the cards and remove them from the wool. Fluff up the pom-poms.

5

6

6 For this badge, make eyes and arms from card and glue them to the pom-pom. Make the back of the badge as shown on page 28.

7

7 You can glue small pom-poms to the basic earring attachment (see page 4), or tie two together to make a hair ornament.

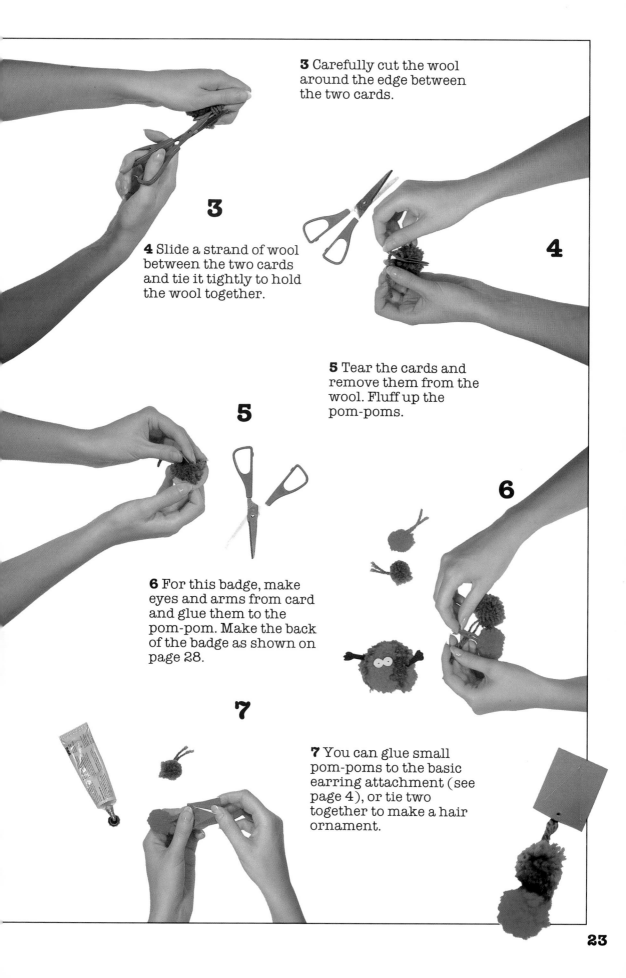

Bead jewellery

These beads make bright, colourful and original jewellery. You can make them any shape you like — round, oval, square, fruit-shaped, even fish-shaped! They are made with a non-bake clay which hardens on exposure to air. This clay is soft and ready to use straight from the packet and can be bought at craft stores.

You will need non-bake clay, cocktail sticks, enamel paints and paint brush, strong thread, paper clips and other fasteners.

1 Roll small amounts of clay between your palms and experiment with making beads of different shapes and sizes.

1

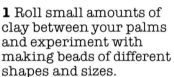

2

2 Make holes through the beads with a dampened cocktail stick.

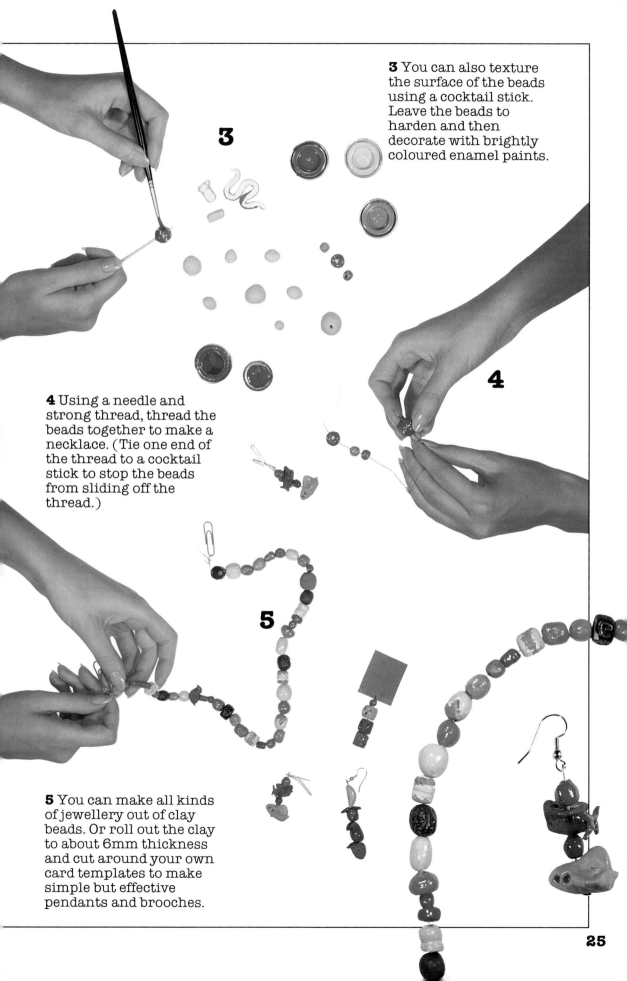

3 You can also texture the surface of the beads using a cocktail stick. Leave the beads to harden and then decorate with brightly coloured enamel paints.

3

4

4 Using a needle and strong thread, thread the beads together to make a necklace. (Tie one end of the thread to a cocktail stick to stop the beads from sliding off the thread.)

5

5 You can make all kinds of jewellery out of clay beads. Or roll out the clay to about 6mm thickness and cut around your own card templates to make simple but effective pendants and brooches.

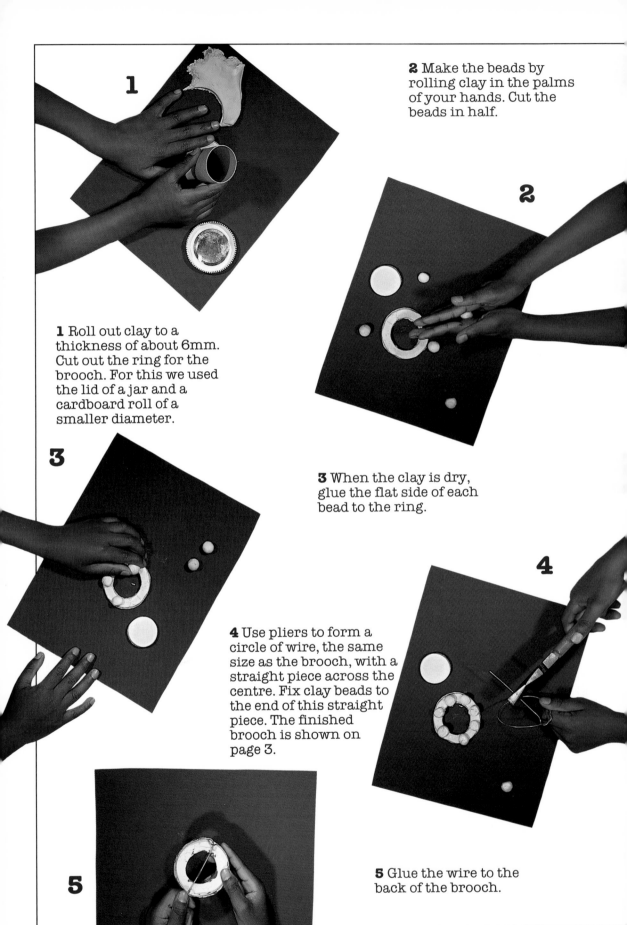

1 Roll out clay to a thickness of about 6mm. Cut out the ring for the brooch. For this we used the lid of a jar and a cardboard roll of a smaller diameter.

2 Make the beads by rolling clay in the palms of your hands. Cut the beads in half.

3 When the clay is dry, glue the flat side of each bead to the ring.

4 Use pliers to form a circle of wire, the same size as the brooch, with a straight piece across the centre. Fix clay beads to the end of this straight piece. The finished brooch is shown on page 3.

5 Glue the wire to the back of the brooch.

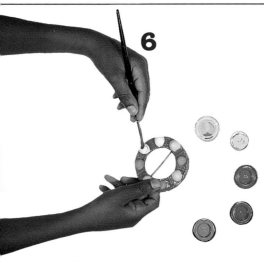

6 When the clay is dry, paint and varnish. Tape a safety pin to the back to act as the fastener.

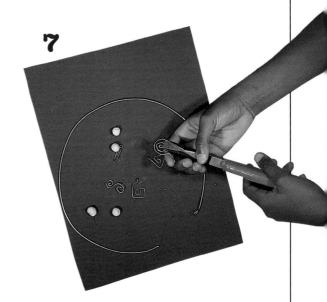

7 With a little practice, you should be able to create lots of interesting shapes out of modelling wire, to make different kinds of jewellery. This Greek-style necklace is made from bent wire shapes and painted clay beads. When you make each wire shape, bend an 'eye' at one end so that the shape can be hung from the choker.

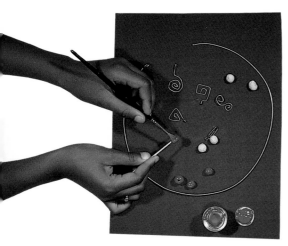

Wire and clay

This more complex jewellery is made from a combination of wire and clay. The brooch is based on a Celtic design and the necklace is based on a traditional Greek design. Turn to page 30 for other ideas of jewellery around the world.

You will need modelling wire, non-bake clay, a pair of pliers, cocktail stick, glue, enamel paints and a paint brush.

Attachments

The parts that make jewellery wearable, like the fastener for a necklace, the pin for a brooch, or the hook for an earring are called findings. They can be bought, quite inexpensively, from craft or other specialist shops. But in most cases, you can substitute home-made attachments.

1 The basic card earring clip shown on page 4 can also be used for pendant earrings. Make a hole with a pencil point at the base of the card, thread a paper clip through it and then attach beads, paper sculpture or bent wire shapes.

2 A circle of card with a safety pin makes a good attachment for a badge or brooch. Here the backing is glued to a pom-pom to turn it into the badge shown on page 23.

3 One of the easiest earring attachments of all is simply a ring of card, cut so that it fits over your ear. Decorate the ring and attach wire shapes or beads.

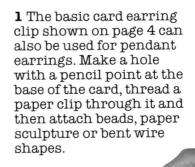

4 This bent wire shape, used in making the Celtic brooch on page 27, also makes a good attachment for a brooch or tie pin. You slide the long piece of wire under a tie or shirt.

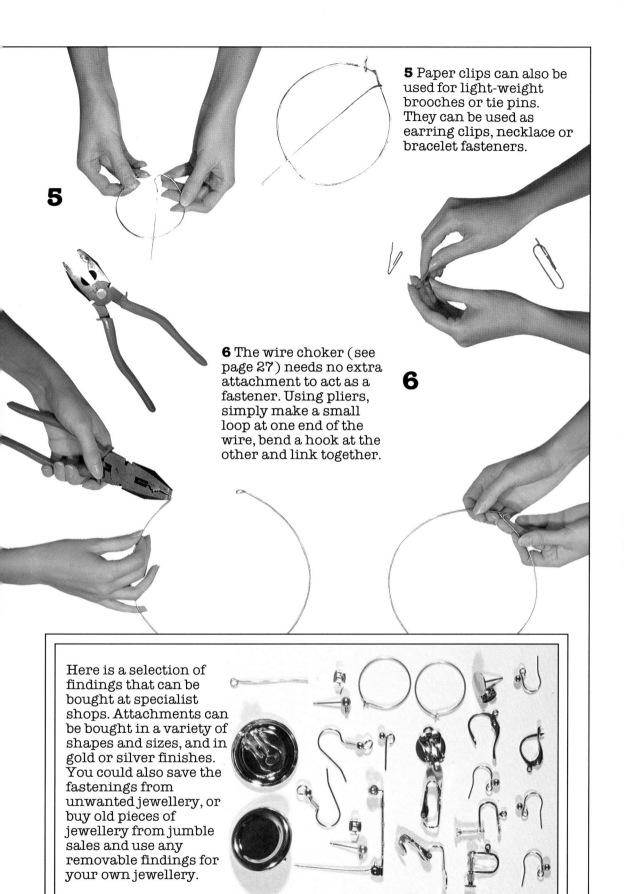

5 Paper clips can also be used for light-weight brooches or tie pins. They can be used as earring clips, necklace or bracelet fasteners.

5

6 The wire choker (see page 27) needs no extra attachment to act as a fastener. Using pliers, simply make a small loop at one end of the wire, bend a hook at the other and link together.

6

Here is a selection of findings that can be bought at specialist shops. Attachments can be bought in a variety of shapes and sizes, and in gold or silver finishes. You could also save the fastenings from unwanted jewellery, or buy old pieces of jewellery from jumble sales and use any removable findings for your own jewellery.

Around the world

When making your own jewellery, you may want to draw the shape before you start or let the design evolve as you go along. Below are some examples of patterns and jewellery from around the world. You can use them as inspiration for your own pieces.

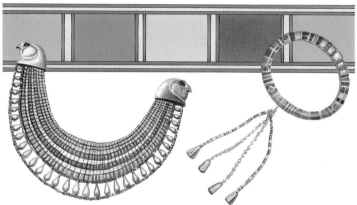

This strip shows an **Egyptian** pattern. The necklace and bracelet are copies of ancient Egyptian jewellery.

This **Greek** pattern can be found on many ancient Greek artefacts. The necklace is also of a traditional Greek design.

Aztec designs and jewellery. These pieces of gold jewellery were once part of the great Aztec treasure.

This strip shows an **Arabic** pattern. The necklace is of a traditional **Indian** design.

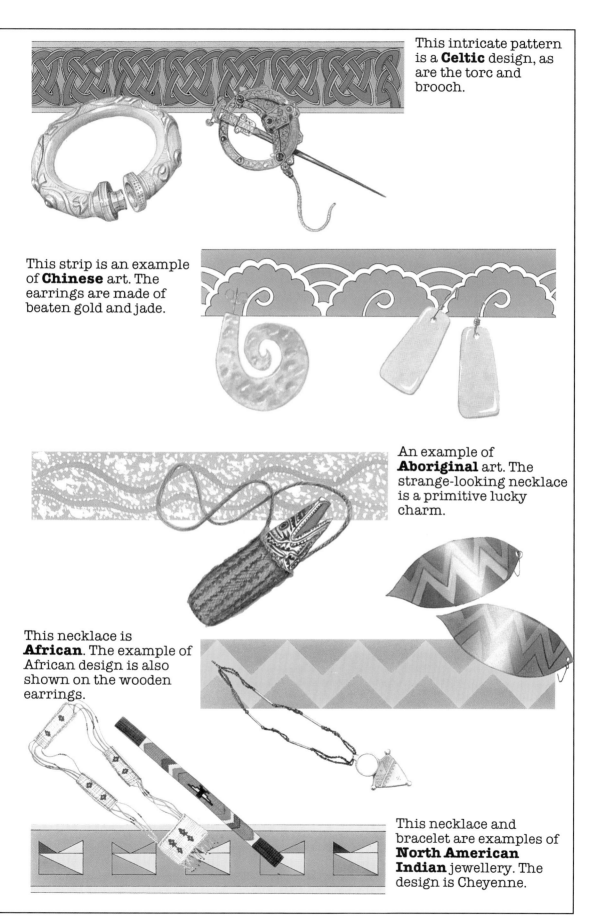

This intricate pattern is a **Celtic** design, as are the torc and brooch.

This strip is an example of **Chinese** art. The earrings are made of beaten gold and jade.

An example of **Aboriginal** art. The strange-looking necklace is a primitive lucky charm.

This necklace is **African**. The example of African design is also shown on the wooden earrings.

This necklace and bracelet are examples of **North American Indian** jewellery. The design is Cheyenne.

Box designs

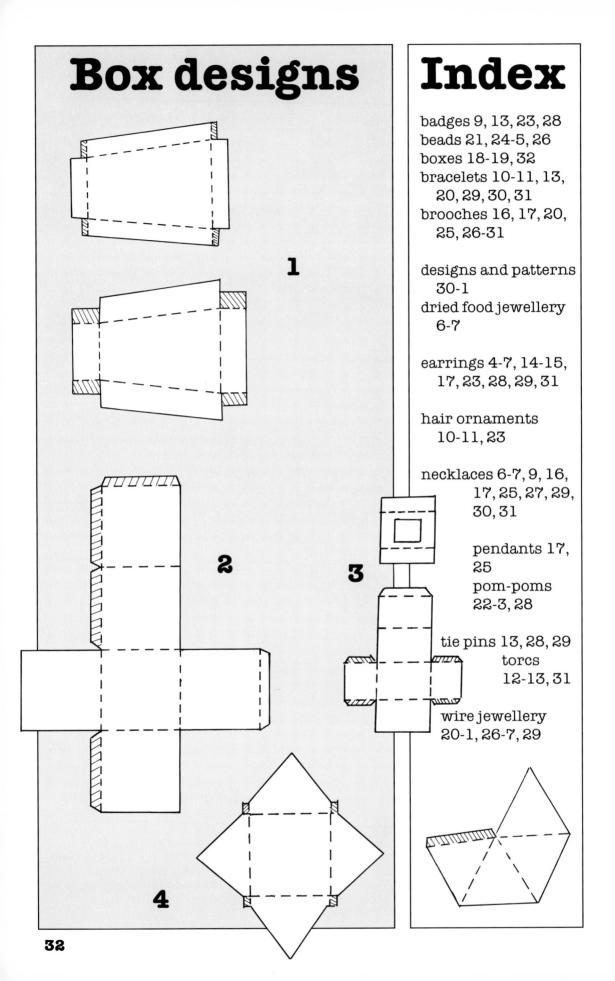

1

2

3

4